DISCOVER

A Whaling Community: Nantucket

WHALE – NANTUOK

by Vickey Herold

Table of Contents

Introduction 2

Chapter 1 What Did a Whaling Community Have? . . . 4

Chapter 2 Why Was Whaling Important? 8

Chapter 3 Why Was Nantucket
a Whaling Community? 14

Conclusion 18

Concept Map 20

Glossary 22

Index 24

Introduction

Nantucket was in the Atlantic Ocean. Nantucket was important long ago. Nantucket was a **whaling community**.

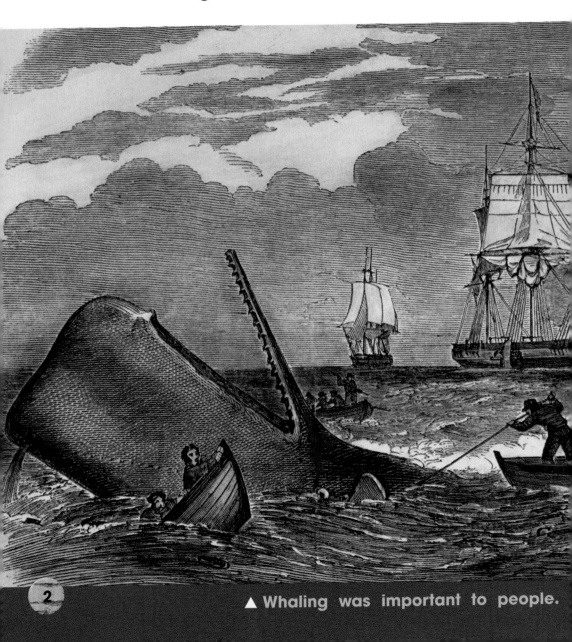

▲ Whaling was important to people.

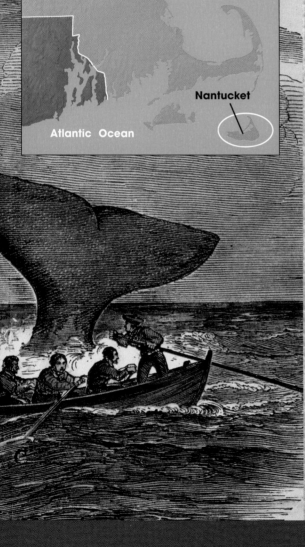

Massachusetts

Massachusetts

Nantucket

Nantucket

Atlantic Ocean

community

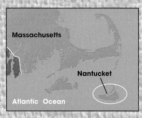

Nantucket

whale hunters

whale oil

whales

whaling

See the Glossary
on page 22.

What Did a Whaling Community Have?

A whaling community had people.

▲ People were in a whaling community.

A whaling community had sailors.

▲ Sailors were in a whaling community.

A whaling community had ships.

▲ Whaling ships were in a whaling community.

A whaling community had **whale hunters**.

▲ Whale hunters were in a whaling community.

Why Was Whaling Important?

People used **whales** for food.

▲ **People had food from whales.**

People used **whale oil**. People used whale oil in candles.

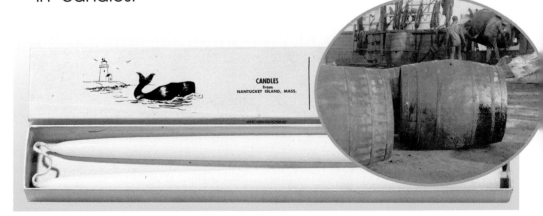

CANDLES
from
NANTUCKET ISLAND, MASS.

▲ **People made candles from whale oil.**

People used whale oil in lamps. People used lamps for light.

People used whale oil in soap.

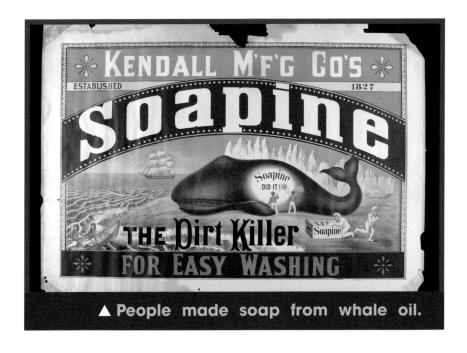

▲ People made soap from whale oil.

People used whale oil in perfume.

▲ People made perfume from whale oil.

People used whales in art.

▲ People made art from whale teeth.

Did You Know?

Whale hunters made art from whales.

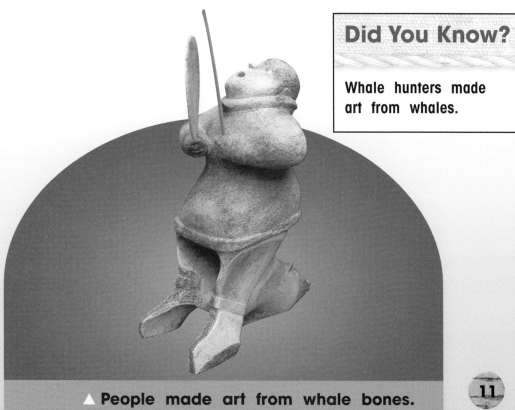

▲ People made art from whale bones.

11

People used whale bones in clothes. People used whale bones in dresses.

▲ **People had dresses with whale bones.**

People used whale bones for tools.

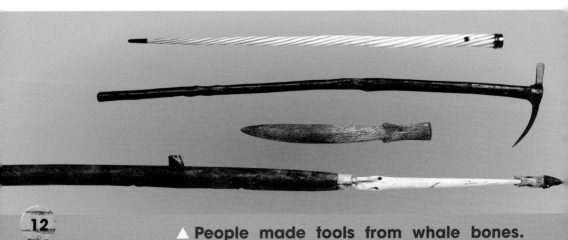

▲ **People made tools from whale bones.**

People used whale bones in umbrellas.

whale bones

▲ People had umbrellas with whale bones.

Why Was Nantucket a Whaling Community?

Nantucket had many whaling ships.

Did You Know?

Nantucket is an island. Whaling ships went to Nantucket.

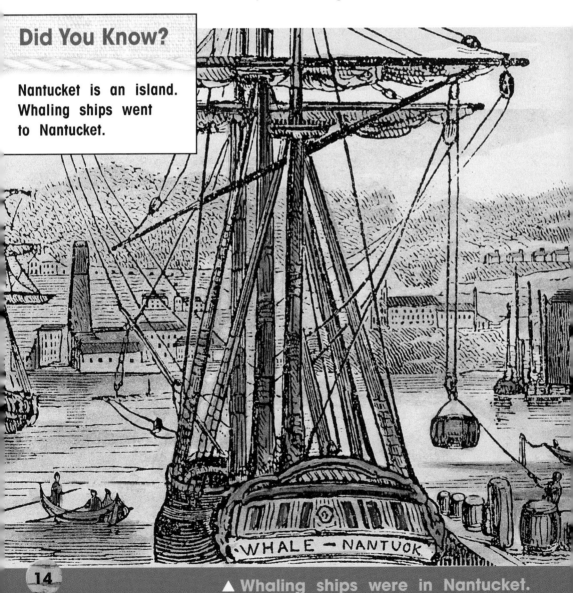

WHALE — NANTUOK.

▲ Whaling ships were in Nantucket.

Nantucket had people. Nantucket had a community.

▲ People were in Nantucket.

Nantucket had many whale hunters.

▲ Whale hunters were in Nantucket.

Nantucket had fishermen.

▲ Fishermen were in Nantucket.

Nantucket had farmers.

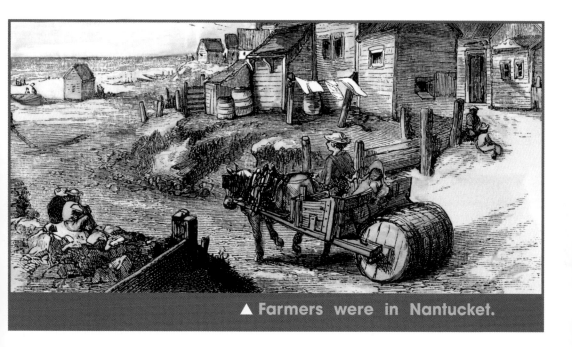

▲ **Farmers were in Nantucket.**

Nantucket had families.

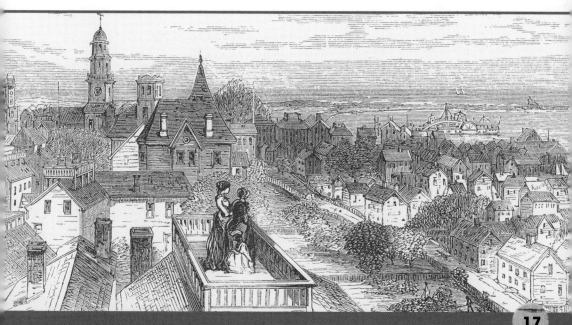

▲ **Families were in Nantucket.**

Conclusion

Nantucket was important for many reasons. Nantucket was a whaling community.

▲ Whaling was important to people.

Concept Map

A Whaling Community: Nantucket

What Did a Whaling Community Have?

people
sailors
ships
whale hunters

Why Was Whaling Important?

People used whales for food.
People used whale oil in candles.
People used whale oil in lamps.
People used whale oil in soap.
People used whale oil in perfume.
People used whales in art.
People used whale bones in clothes.
People used whale bones for tools.
People used whale bones in umbrellas.

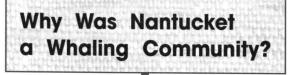

Why Was Nantucket a Whaling Community?

had whaling ships
had people
had whale hunters
had fishermen
had farmers
had families

Glossary

community a place where people live and work

*A whaling **community** had people.*

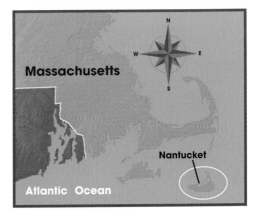

Nantucket an island that is part of Massachusetts

Nantucket was in the Atlantic Ocean.

whale hunters people who hunt whales

*Nantucket had many **whale hunters**.*

whale oil a greasy liquid from whales

*People used **whale oil** in candles.*

whales very big animals that live in the ocean

*People used **whales** for food.*

whaling hunting whales

*A **whaling** community had whale hunters.*

Index

art, 11

Atlantic Ocean, 2

candles, 8

clothes, 12

community, 2, 4–7, 15, 18

families, 17

farmers, 17

fishermen, 16

food, 8

lamps, 9

light, 9

Nantucket, 2, 14–18

people, 4, 8–13, 15

perfume, 10

sailors, 5

ships, 6, 14

soap, 10

tools, 12

umbrellas, 13

whale bones, 12–13

whale hunters, 7, 16

whale oil, 8–10

whales, 8, 11

whaling, 2, 4–7, 14, 18